YOU CAN SAVE THE PLANET

50 WAYS YOU CAN MAKE A DIFFERENCE

YOU CAN SAVE THE PLANET

50 WAYS YOU CAN MAKE A DIFFERENCE

Written by JACQUIE WINES

Illustrated by SARAH HORNE

SCHOLASTIC

Contents

HELP!

Human beings have damaged or destroyed a third of Earth's natural wealth—its wildlife, its forests, its rivers, and its seas. However, the most serious impact of our actions is on climate change. Scientists overwhelmingly agree that Earth is getting warmer, and they believe that human activity is making temperatures rise more quickly than they might otherwise.

Climate change is probably the most serious, long-term threat our planet is facing. The evidence of it is all around us. The sea ice in the Arctic has shrunk by more than 386,000 miles^2 (1 million km^2); all over the globe glaciers are melting; the ten hottest years on record have all occurred since 1991; and sea levels are rising, which increases the likelihood of flooding and death.

On the following pages you will see evidence of the damage that climate change is causing throughout the world.

In addition to the extreme weather conditions that bring drought and hurricanes, the increasing temperatures are causing the vast sheets of ice that cover the poles to melt. The Greenland ice sheet is the size of Europe and is melting faster than scientists anticipated. If it were to melt completely, sea levels around the world would rise 20.3 ft (6.2 m) and most of Earth's coastal cities could be destroyed.

This damage to the planet is happening because the planet's resources are being used up—in other words, we are being too greedy and too wasteful. We buy vast quantities of unwanted things. We bury billions of tons of garbage in holes in the ground. We pump enormous amounts of dangerous gases into the atmosphere, and we pour sewage and toxic chemicals into the seas and oceans.

Some scientists say that if we don't act now to reduce climate change, in ten years' time it will be too late to save the planet. So it's up to you to act. You need to take responsibility for the planet's future. Look at the way you and your family live, and make changes that will ensure your household is "greener" and more friendly to the environment.

In this book you will find 50 simple but effective things you can do to reduce the damage being done to the planet. This book will help you to make the right changes and the right choices.

Earth's future . . .
your future . . . is in your hands.
Go to work.

Climate change is threatening polar bears with starvation by shortening their hunting season, according to a study by scientists.

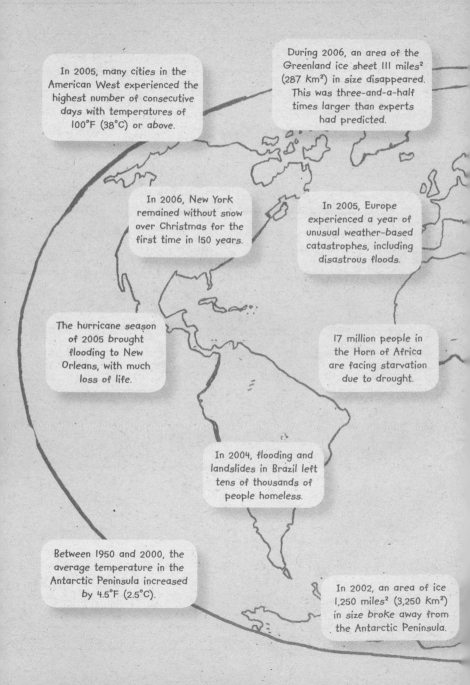

In 2005, many cities in the American West experienced the highest number of consecutive days with temperatures of 100°F (38°C) or above.

During 2006, an area of the Greenland ice sheet 111 miles² (287 km²) in size disappeared. This was three-and-a-half times larger than experts had predicted.

In 2006, New York remained without snow over Christmas for the first time in 150 years.

In 2005, Europe experienced a year of unusual weather-based catastrophes, including disastrous floods.

The hurricane season of 2005 brought flooding to New Orleans, with much loss of life.

17 million people in the Horn of Africa are facing starvation due to drought.

In 2004, flooding and landslides in Brazil left tens of thousands of people homeless.

Between 1950 and 2000, the average temperature in the Antarctic Peninsula increased by 4.5°F (2.5°C).

In 2002, an area of ice 1,250 miles² (3,250 km²) in size broke away from the Antarctic Peninsula.

The average temperature in western Siberia has increased by 5.4°F (3°C) in the last 40 years.

In 2003, record temperatures across Europe were considered responsible for approximately 35,000 deaths.

In 2004, Japan was hit by ten typhoons. This was the highest number recorded in one year in the country's history.

In one area of the Himalayas called Tien Shan, 400 glaciers are believed to have shrunk by 25% in the last 50 years.

Thirty-five islands make up the Kiribati islands. Two have disappeared beneath the sea as a result of rising sea levels. The remaining 33 are likely to follow.

In July 2005, Mumbai in India experienced the heaviest rain any city in India has ever suffered in one day. During a 24-hour period 37 in (94 cm) of rain fell.

Between 2002 and 2005, bush-fires raged in Australia as a result of abnormally low rainfall.

In New Zealand, three-quarters of all the glaciers that scientists have examined show signs of shrinking.

Start helping your planet by making changes at home.

It's up to you to find out how energy-efficient your household is. You need to assess how wasteful the members of your family are. Find out where you can make changes and insist on improvements.

Chapter One

Do You Live In A Green House?

No. 1: Assess Your Excesses

Find out how many energy crimes are being committed in your household every day. Make a note of the following:

ENERGY DIARY

• I have taken a look and our attic is/is not insulated.

• I tested each window in our house for drafts by holding a feather in front of it and seeing whether it fluttered. .... windows had drafts.

• We have .... lightbulbs in this house. .... of them are energy-efficient, fluorescent bulbs.

• I walked around the house and .... lights had been left on in rooms that were not being used.

• When I checked, ... electrical appliances in the house were on standby.

• The heating/air-conditioning was set to .... , but unfortunately .... windows were open.

• I checked the washing machine and the dishwasher when they were last used and they were full/half full.

• .... taps in the house were dripping.

No. 2: Switch It Off

Did you know that a color
TV left on standby can use
85% of the energy it uses
when it is actually on?

A DVD player left on
standby uses almost as
much electricity as when
it is playing a disc.

Every gadget in your
house that is left on
standby wastes energy. You can often tell if an appliance
is on standby because you'll see a little red light on it
glowing. Many appliances go to standby if you use a
remote control to switch them off. You might not think
a little red light can do much harm, but it is costing
millions of dollars in wasted energy.

OVER TO YOU

• Check every appliance in your house, including TVs,
computers, cell phone chargers, and DVD players. When
an appliance is not being used, it should be switched off
at the socket on the wall or unplugged completely.

• Tell your parents they could save up to 13% on their
electricity bill by doing this simple thing. They will be
saving money as well as saving the planet.

No.3: Choose The Right Light

Check out every light and lamp in your house. How many of them have energy-efficient lightbulbs?

Compact fluorescent, spiral lightbulbs last ten times longer than standard incandescent lightbulbs and use 66% less energy.

Point this out to anybody who buys another box of "old-fashioned" energy-wasting lightbulbs, and rant at anyone who leaves on lights that are not needed. They'll soon get the message.

No.4: Washday Decisions

Turning on the washing machine just to wash your jeans or a football jersey wastes water and electricity. And did you know that all the detergents you use pollute the water system?

Copy out this list of rules for your household and make washday a more eco-friendly occasion:

WASHDAY RULES

• If clothes aren't really dirty we will use a cooler wash. This saves electricity, because 90% of the energy used by a washing machine is used in heating the water.

• We will only switch on the washing machine when it is completely full.

• We will wash single items by hand.

• We will use environmentally friendly detergents.

• We will use less detergents and we will NOT use fabric softeners.

• We will go easy on stain removers.

• We will try to keep our clothes cleaner so we can wear them for longer without washing them.

No.5: Get Out The Rubber Gloves

An eco-warrior's life is never easy. Sometimes you will need to weigh the pros and cons of an issue in order to make a sensible choice. Take dishwashers: There are times when it makes eco-sense to turn them off, and times to use them.

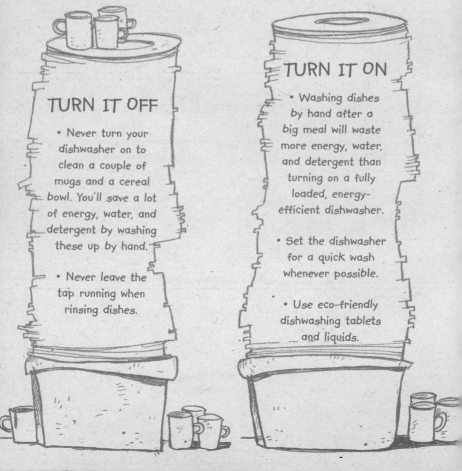

TURN IT OFF

• Never turn your dishwasher on to clean a couple of mugs and a cereal bowl. You'll save a lot of energy, water, and detergent by washing these up by hand.

• Never leave the tap running when rinsing dishes.

TURN IT ON

• Washing dishes by hand after a big meal will waste more energy, water, and detergent than turning on a fully loaded, energy-efficient dishwasher.

• Set the dishwasher for a quick wash whenever possible.

• Use eco-friendly dishwashing tablets and liquids.

No.6: Check That Thermostat And Love Your Layers

Adjusting the temperature on the thermostat of your heating and air-conditioning units by only 3°F (1.5°C) can reduce the greenhouse gases your household produces by up to a ton. So take a look at the thermostat and check whether you really need the air-conditioning that cold or the heating that hot.

Find out about greenhouse gases and the effect they are having on our planet on the next page.

Another really simple but effective thing to do is dust or vacuum the surfaces of all the radiators in your house. This increases their efficiency by improving the flow of heat.

Duh!

If the thermostat for your heating or air-conditioning is near a window, make sure the window is shut. Otherwise the thermostat will have the wrong impression of the temperature in the house.

Have you ever noticed anyone in your house opening windows while the heat is on full blast? If you spy such scandalous, energy-wasting behavior going on, take action.

Alternatively, have you spotted someone wearing a T-shirt turning up the heat? Tell the guilty party to put on some layers if they are feeling cold—it's 100% greener.

No. 7: Make Your Own Detergent

Keeping a house clean can make the planet dirty. Polishes, disinfectants, window-cleaning products, and kitchen and bathroom cleansers pollute the environment. Just throwing away the empty containers of these products increases the amount of garbage in landfill sites.

Why not use vinegar and baking soda to clean the bathtub, sinks, and kitchen surfaces? Dip the sponge in vinegar and wipe. Use the baking soda to scour the surface clean. Rinse the surface with clean water. Try mixing equal amounts of water and vinegar and use it to clean windows.

No. 8: Don't Waste Water

Without water there would be no life on Earth. Every plant, animal, and insect needs water. Even though 70% of Earth's surface is covered with water, only 2.5% is fresh water we can drink. Much of this fresh water isn't easy for us to reach, as it is frozen in glaciers and ice caps, or buried underground. So we need to start saving every drop of the drinking water in our taps right now.

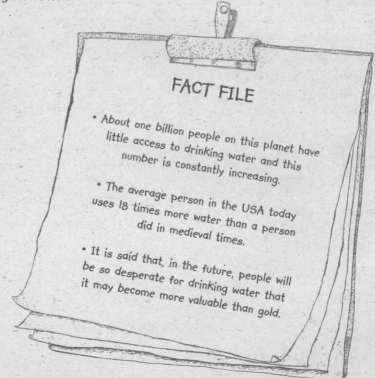

FACT FILE

• About one billion people on this planet have little access to drinking water and this number is constantly increasing.

• The average person in the USA today uses 18 times more water than a person did in medieval times.

• It is said that, in the future, people will be so desperate for drinking water that it may become more valuable than gold.

OVER TO YOU

• Never leave taps running. Up to 2 gal (7.5 L) of water can run out of a tap in one minute. Wash your hands in a basin of water, not under a running tap. Turning off a tap while you clean your teeth will save up to 3.7 gal (14 L) of water.

• Nag your parents to repair any dripping faucets.

• Don't flush the toilet when you have just had a pee. Did you know an average family of four people can flush 100 gal (375 L) of water down the toilet every day? Write this out and hang it by the toilet:

> If it's yellow, let it mellow,
> If it's brown, flush it down.

• Never let anyone flush the toilet when they have thrown a tissue in it.

• Having a short shower uses a third of the water used taking a bath.

GREENHOUSE GASES

Greenhouse gases are a group of gases that scientists believe are affecting the climate of our planet. The main greenhouse gases are water vapor, carbon dioxide (CO_2), methane, and ozone. Many greenhouse gases occur naturally, some are man-made, but all are increased by burning fuels such as coal and oil. Burning rain forests also releases millions of tons of greenhouse gases into the air every year.

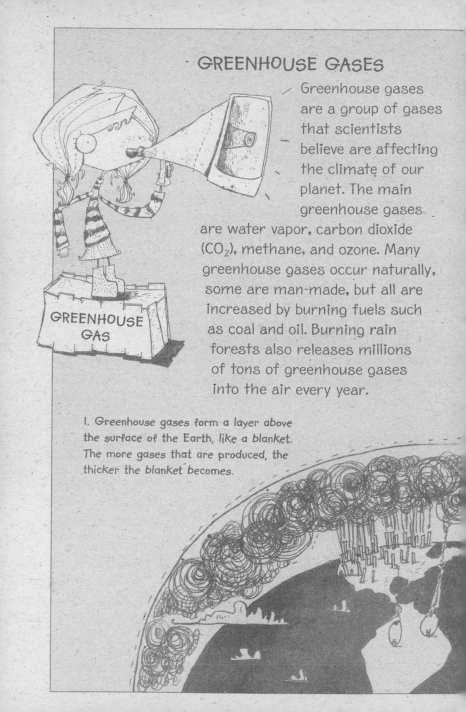

GREENHOUSE GAS

1. Greenhouse gases form a layer above the surface of the Earth, like a blanket. The more gases that are produced, the thicker the blanket becomes.

THE GREENHOUSE EFFECT

The rise in temperature that Earth experiences as a result of the buildup of the greenhouse gases is called the greenhouse effect (illustrated below). Greenhouse gases form a layer in the atmosphere above Earth's surface. This layer acts like a blanket and traps the heat from the Sun. Without these gases, the Sun's energy would escape back into space. Instead, the temperature of the planet increases. The more gases that build up, the greater the effect will be.

THE GREENHOUSE EFFECT

2. Heat from the Sun reaches Earth. Some is reflected back into space, but some is trapped by the greenhouse gases.

3. As a result, the temperature of the planet increases.

Whether you have plants growing in window boxes or in pots on a balcony, or a garden at home, or an area at your school where there are plants and trees, you need to check how eco-friendly the gardeners around you are. Do they really have green thumbs? Or do they waste water, and kill weeds and pests with poisons that pollute the planet?

Make sure the plants and wildlife that live around you have a chemical-free environment in which to thrive.

Chapter Two

The Great Green Outdoors

No.9: Watering The Plants

Did you know that the amount of water we have on Earth has always been the same? In other words, there is no more water available now than there was when dinosaurs were around; it simply gets recycled by nature over and over again. As there is no way of getting new water, we need to conserve the supply we have.

In the developed world many people waste water. Make sure your family is not guilty of this.

OVER TO YOU

• Stop anyone you see using a hose to water plants. A hose uses huge amounts of water. Use a watering can instead.

• Leave out buckets to catch rainwater and use these to water your plants. If you have a garden, perhaps you could persuade your family to buy a big rain barrel to collect water.

• Choose plants for your window boxes, pots, or garden that like dry conditions, if that's what you have in your area. Why not plant some lavender or sage?

ECO-BLUNDER

Here's a story that demonstrates how careful governments must be with water strategy.

The Aral Sea, in Kazakhstan, Central Asia, was once the fourth largest lake in the world. However, in the 1960s the local government decided it would be a good idea to change local prairie land into cotton fields. To do this they needed lots of water, so they built canals to divert two rivers that had previously flowed into the Aral Sea.

The lake's water began to dry up and became very salty. The fish in it died, so the local fishermen could no longer earn a living. The wind blew the salt onto the land, so crops could not grow. Although the government had tried to make things better, their actions made the situation very much worse.

No. 10: Plant A Tree

Planet Earth once had many more trees than it has today. Humans have cut them down in order to make room for towns and cities and to create fields in which to grow food. Today, forests are disappearing fast. Clearing forests and burning trees is one of the major causes of greenhouse gases in the atmosphere. Here are some shocking facts:

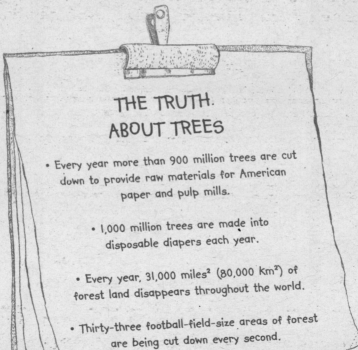

THE TRUTH ABOUT TREES

- Every year more than 900 million trees are cut down to provide raw materials for American paper and pulp mills.

- 1,000 million trees are made into disposable diapers each year.

- Every year, 31,000 miles² (80,000 km²) of forest land disappears throughout the world.

- Thirty-three football-field-size areas of forest are being cut down every second.

So does it really matter that all these trees are disappearing?

Yes. The main reason that trees are so important to the planet is that they help us breathe. They clean the air by soaking up poisonous gases like carbon monoxide, sulfur dioxide, and nitrogen dioxide. One tree can filter up to 60 lbs (27 kg) of pollutants from the air each year.

Furthermore, trees give off the oxygen that we need to breathe. One mature tree can provide enough oxygen for a family of four to breathe for a whole year.

Did you know that trees are the longest-living organism in the world, and can grow for hundreds of years?

Yes, but with pollution increasing at the rate it is, trees planted in cities are often surviving for fewer than ten years.

OVER TO YOU

• Get planting. To choose which species, look at the trees in your area, as some may grow better than others. Get permission to plant a tree at school, in a local park, or in a garden. Why not start by planting apple or tomato seeds in a pot?

• Don't forget to recycle paper, too (see page 63).

No. 11: Grow Your Own

It is seriously good fun to grow food yourself and it ensures zero pesticides are involved in getting good food on your plate.

How about growing some delicious cherry tomatoes? You don't need a garden to plant them in, just some pots on a sunny windowsill.

The best time of year to plant tomatoes is towards the end of April when winter is over.

1. Scoop some seeds out of a cherry tomato you are given for lunch. Rinse the seeds in water and leave them to dry.

2. Fill empty yogurt containers with some compost. Push a tomato seed into the center of each container just below the surface of the compost and cover it. Water the compost lightly.

3. Label your containers clearly (so no one throws them away by mistake!) and leave them on a sunny windowsill. Check them every day, watering as needed so that the compost always feels moist when you touch it. However,

be careful not to overwater them. After about a week, you should see tiny shoots appear.

4. After about four weeks, the shoots will have grown into tiny plants. Lift them out of the containers gently, taking as many roots as possible and being careful not to damage them. Transfer the shoots to large flowerpots full of seed compost, gently firming them into position.

5. Keep checking and watering your tomato plants (by this time you may need to water them twice a day). After a few weeks, you should see some flowers appearing. These flowers will eventually fall off, leaving tiny green tomatoes.

6. When your tomatoes are bright red and feel slightly squishy, they are ripe and ready to pick and eat.

No. 12: How Green Is Your Mower?

Here's a shocker—a gasoline mower running for a year can produce the same amount of pollution as 40 cars on the road for a year.

Another huge problem with lawn mowers is accidental fuel spills. Did you know that if all the fuel spilled when people refill their mowers was put together in one pool, it would cause as much damage as a slick from an oil tanker disaster?

So if you have a lovely lawn and the time comes to cut it, make sure your family buys an electric mower . . . or better still, a mechanical one—go on, get pushing for your planet!

No.13: Protect Local Birds

As cities grow, and fields and park areas are built over, and grass disappears under patios, paving, and decking, many birds have found themselves homeless and hungry.

OVER TO YOU

Here are some of the ways you can help the birds that live near you.

• Provide your bird pals something they can use as a bath—birds need to keep their feathers clean to keep warm. Put out an old baking tray or a large pottery bowl and fill it with clean water.

• Build a bird a home using a large, empty, plastic milk container with holes the size of an egg cut through them. Put some shredded paper or straw inside the container to be used as bedding.

• If you have a garden, tell your family to think twice about digging up the lawn and replacing it with gravel, a patio, or decking. All the insects and worms that lived in that grass will be killed and garden birds will go hungry.

• Don't use pesticides on plants and insects. Birds may eat them.

Birds are happy to be offered most kitchen leftovers, as well as seeds and nuts. So never let anyone in your household throw away any leftover food without checking this list first:

- cakes
- cookies
- bread
- crumbled cheese
- pasta
- cooked rice
- pastries
- bacon rind

- old fruit
- potatoes
- unsalted nuts
- fat from meat
- bones

(Do NOT give birds salted nuts or dried coconut.)

Put up a bird feeder on a balcony or in a garden area. Make sure it is somewhere out of the reach of hungry cats.

Local birds will soon identify your feeder as a reliable source of food, so don't forget to keep feeding them through the winter.

No.14: Make A Composter

A lot of kitchen and garden waste is organic matter, which, in other words, is stuff that was once alive. If you were to make a heap of it outdoors, in just a few days it would be visited by bacteria, algae, and fungi, which will cause it to rot. Worms, beetles, and maggots make a tasty meal of all the rotting matter, leaving lots of tiny little pieces that we call compost. Pretty GROSS, but compost is a very good fertilizer for gardens.

OVER TO YOU

• Build or buy a compost container and put it in the garden. Composts need to be warm and damp, so a sunny, sheltered spot is ideal.

• A composter loves all grass and plant cuttings from your garden. It loves the peelings you have from fruit and vegetables, but don't add meat, cheese, or fish, or you may encourage rats into your garden.

• Keep a container into which the things listed on page 39 can be emptied, ready for composting. Check no one is putting these things in the garbage can instead.

• When the composter collection box is full, take it out into the garden and empty it into the composter. Two-thirds of the household garbage we put in our trash cans could be composted. Copy the list to the right and stick it on your fridge to remind people what goes in the compost box.

• Finally, feel free to pee on your compost heap, but only occasionally. Some people think this is a really good idea, although others think it makes the compost rather acidic.

FEED ME
• grass cuttings
• hair cuttings
• hay
• straw
• hedge trimmings
• non-colored paper
• tea bags
• vegetable peelings
• leftover vegetables
• leftover fruit
• coffee grounds
• cut-up newspaper
• cardboard

Why not buy your household a wormery or add worms to your compost heap? Worms love to eat tea bags, coffee grounds, and soggy cardboard. They even like newspaper when it has been torn into tasty strips. Watch while your worms turn your household waste into wonderful compost that will help your garden grow.

Did you know the average person in the United States produces more than six pounds of trash every day? All that garbage has to be put somewhere. Most of it is buried underground in landfill sites. This means our planet is in danger of becoming one big garbage dump.

The easiest way to deal with the huge problem of garbage is sensible shopping—buy less stuff, which means less waste packaging and less waste to throw away.

Chapter Three
Shopping For The Planet

No. 15: Shopping Lists

It's essential to monitor your household's weekly shopping lists and make sure that it only includes things that will last, rather than things that will soon be thrown away. Here are some classic examples:

BUY-TO-THROW LIST

- disposable diapers
- plastic pens
- plastic razors
- paper towels
- paper tissues
- plastic food bags
- paper tablecloths and napkins, plastic plates and straws

BUY-TO-KEEP LIST

- cloth diapers
- one good pen
- a non-disposable razor
- washable dishcloths
- linen handkerchiefs
- plastic food containers
- washable or wipe-down tablecloths, china plates, linen napkins

No. 16: Say No To Bottled Water

Don't be fooled into thinking bottled water is better for you than tap water. Here's why:

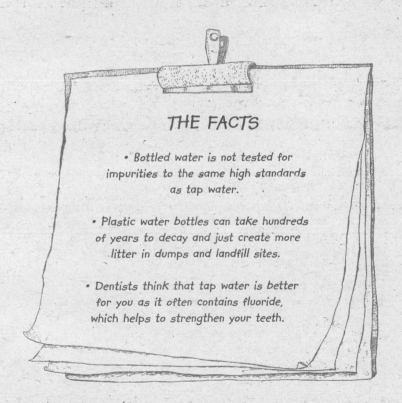

THE FACTS

- Bottled water is not tested for impurities to the same high standards as tap water.

- Plastic water bottles can take hundreds of years to decay and just create more litter in dumps and landfill sites.

- Dentists think that tap water is better for you as it often contains fluoride, which helps to strengthen your teeth.

No. 17: Shopping For Greens

Next time someone heads to the supermarket, get them to read and agree to the shopping contract shown below.

OUR FAMILY SHOPPING CONTRACT

• Our household will do only one BIG shop a week.
This will encourage us not to buy unwanted food, and we will use less gas getting to and from the supermarket.

• Whenever possible we will choose organic foods farmed without the use of chemicals.
This is better for the Earth and is probably better for us, too.

• Whenever possible we'll buy food from local producers.
It uses up less fuel to transport this food to the supermarket.

• We will buy fruit and vegetables in season.
("In season" means at the time of year they naturally grow.)
We check the labels to see what country they have come from and resist stuff that has been flown halfway around the world.

No.18: Eat Fruit, Don't Drink Juices

Ready-made fruit juices contain lots of sugar, but, worse still, the production of fruit juices requires both huge amounts of packaging and huge amounts of water.

By eating real fruit, you will save your teeth, save water, save energy, and prevent even more garbage ending up in landfill sites.

OVER TO YOU

• Buy organic fruit from local farms or farmers' markets. This cuts down both on the pesticides polluting the planet and the gas used in transport.
• If you only like fruit in the form of juice, dig out the juicer you never use and make your own.
• Don't forget to compost all your peelings and any fruit that gets overripe and too old to eat (see page 38).

No.19: Buy In Bulk

This book has taught you to buy only the things you need, and never to buy more than you need. However, when you buy essential items, it is a good idea to buy them in the largest containers you can find. This is called buying in bulk. Buying in bulk means fewer car trips to the shops, which means less gas and pollution. It means less packaging, too. Plus the good news is, bulk-buying is often cheaper.

It's soooo much better buying small packets of food, because there's less waste.

Duh!
Actually, bulk-buying reduces packaging, not the other way around. For example, one large cereal box is made from less cardboard than two small ones. Squash the boxes flat and measure them if you like.

However, steer clear of big bags of individually wrapped sweets or potato chips. These have extra packaging. The same goes for bottles of water or other multi-buy goods that are bound together with plastic wrapping.

No.20: Fast Food Is Forbidden

We all know by now that fast food isn't good for us, but did you know it isn't very good for the planet, either?

Fast-food restaurants often individually wrap their food. Just think of all the packaging you get when you buy a burger—the burger is in a box, the fries in a bag, the drink is in a Styrofoam cup, the salt, the pepper, and the sauces come in packets and there's often paper napkins, plastic cutlery, and a straw all thrown into another big bag so you can carry it all.

And what do people do the minute they leave the shop? They throw away all the packaging—hopefully in the bin, but sometimes on the pavement.

Plastic packaging material does not decompose for hundreds of years (see page 56) and is cluttering up our landfill sites. Meanwhile, garbage left on our streets attracts rats that may spread disease.

OVER TO YOU

• Try to eat in cafés and restaurants where food is served on a china plate with metal cutlery. These can be used again and again. If you can't resist fast food, put the packaging into your recycling bin, and at least say no to the free plastic toy—you will just end up throwing it away.

No.21: Dry-Cleaning Ban

When you send clothes to the dry cleaners, chemicals are used to get out the stains. Unfortunately these chemicals (known as volatile organic compounds or VOCs) make stains on our planet that are harder to remove. In fact, they turn our skies brown. Check out these dirty facts:

DIRTY FACTS ABOUT DRY CLEANING

- VOCs mix with nitrogen oxides in the atmosphere, where they react to form ozone at ground level. This appears as a brownish haze.

- The chemical tetrachloroethylene that is used in dry cleaning can cause cancer in animals.

- When you pick up your clothes from the dry cleaners they may still retain low levels of tetrachloroethylene that you might breathe in when you wear them.

- Dry cleaners put clean clothes on metal hangers and put them in plastic bags—really wasteful!

So, if anyone in your family is about to buy an item of clothing that is dry-clean only, make sure they know the effect it will have on the planet.

No.22: Don't Be A Gadget Geek

New gadgets and toys are fun to play with ... well, they are at first. But are they really useful?

Make a spreadsheet that lists each unused gadget in your household. Sit your family down and get them to confess when they last used each item.

Use your spreadsheet to work out which gadgets are no longer used by your family. Don't throw them away, but instead take them to a flea market, a thrift store, or perhaps sell them on eBay. You don't want someone else buying a new useless gadget if they can take yours.

GADGET	LAST USED
Toaster	
Electric carving knife	
Foot or face spa	
Floor-polishing machine	
Leaf blower	
Juicer	
Plug-in grill	
Slow cooker	
Electronic toys	
Electronic gym equipment	

Finally, make your family promise to think hard before buying gadgets that may end up lying around the house unused.

No.23: Use Energy-Efficient Appliances

If your parents are about to set off and buy a new household appliance, insist on going with them—you have a serious job to do.

Make sure they pick energy-efficient appliances. For example, using an energy-efficient fridge could save half a ton of CO_2 a year compared to an older model.

You should be able to find out specific information on how energy-efficient an appliance is in the shop before you buy. Look out for an energy-efficiency logo or a label on the appliance detailing its energy consumption.

Failing this, ask the store assistant if he can provide this information, and don't take no for an answer.

Always ensure that any appliance in your house is not only energy-efficient but that it is being used efficiently by your family. For example, your fridge could be responsible for about 20% of your household's electricity use.

Take a look at your fridge and fill in this questionnaire:

FRIDGE QUESTIONNAIRE

	YES	NO
Is our fridge set to the correct temperature as stated in the manual?	☐	☐
Is our fridge kept well stocked? (Did you know a half-full fridge or freezer uses more energy than a full one?)	☐	☐
Is the fridge located in a good place? (It will use more energy if it is placed next to a radiator or the oven.)	☐	☐
Is the fridge defrosted regularly? (If not, the freezer compartment door may not shut properly, and this means the fridge will not work efficiently.)	☐	☐

If your family buys a new fridge or freezer, always make sure the old one is disposed of responsibly.

If there is nothing wrong with it, see if someone else wants it.

Chlorofluorocarbons, or CFCs, are chemicals used in refrigeration and air-conditioning units and products such as aerosol sprays. When they get into the air, CFCs destroy ozone (see below). Removing CFCs from fridges requires special equipment. If your fridge is really old, take it to your local trash and recycling center or have it collected by your town so that it can be disposed of properly.

OZONE LAYER

The ozone layer is made of a form of oxygen. It is found about 9 to 22 miles (15 to 35 km) above Earth's surface. It helps to protect our planet from the Sun's more harmful rays, and especially from ultraviolet (UV) radiation, which causes skin cancer.

Every time even a small amount of the ozone layer is lost, more UV light from the Sun can reach Earth. This may change the planet's climate by increasing its temperature.

OZONE LAYER

No. 24: Give Green Gifts

Here's a project for truly committed eco-warriors . . . on holidays and birthdays, resist the temptation to ask for loads of presents. Ask yourself how much you really appreciated all the things people bought you last year. Chances are you will have forgotten, broken, or gotten bored with at least some of the gifts.

This year don't get throwaway presents. Ask for a trip to the zoo, a football game, or the movies.

Oh, and don't tarnish your green halo by showering your loved ones with offerings either. Give good deeds. Wash your dad's car. Tidy Granny's garden. Take out the garbage.

Our planet has a "finite" amount of resources. This means that they are limited and that we can't replace the materials we have taken from the planet with new ones. All the metal, gems, coal, and oil we take out of the ground every day took millions of years to form. When they are used up, there won't be any more for us to take.

This is why it's so important that we don't buy anything we don't need, we don't waste, that we repair and reuse as much as possible, and failing all else, we recycle absolutely everything we can.

Chapter Four

Reduce, Reuse, Repair, Recycle

No.25: Make A Decay Diary

To make sure people understand just how long garbage in landfill sites takes to biodegrade, perform the following experiment. Find a piece of land on which you have permission to dig. Make a hole and bury some or all of the following items:

- an apple
- a banana
- eggshells
- a tea bag
- an old shoe
- a woolly hat or glove
- a toilet paper tube

- a tin can
- a newspaper advertisement
- a potato chip bag
- a plastic bottle
- a plastic bag

Visit your experiment site regularly. Uncover the items and notice what changes have occurred between visits. Write down how long each item takes to decompose.

Check out the following depressing decay data:

- a sheet of paper will take 2 to 5 months to decay.
- an orange peel will take 6 months to decay.
- a milk carton will take 5 years to decay.
- a cigarette butt will take 10 years to decay.
- **a tin can will take 100 years to decay.**
- an aluminum can will take 200 to 500 years to decay.
- a plastic six-pack holder will take 450 years to decay.
- a plastic bag will take 500 to 1,000 years to decay.
- **a Styrofoam cup will NEVER decay!**

No.26: Recycle Glass Bottles, Cans, And Jars

Huge furnaces all over the world can each produce more than a million glass bottles and jars every day. Think how many of those containers are littering our planet. It is essential to recycle all the glass bottles and jars that come into your house.

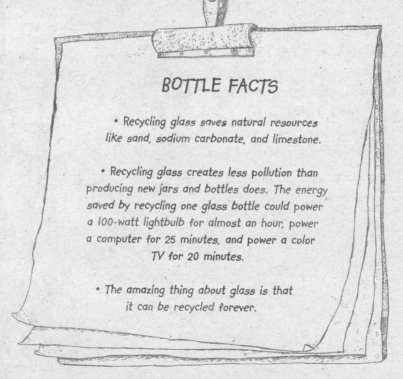

BOTTLE FACTS

• Recycling glass saves natural resources like sand, sodium carbonate, and limestone.

• Recycling glass creates less pollution than producing new jars and bottles does. The energy saved by recycling one glass bottle could power a 100-watt lightbulb for almost an hour, power a computer for 25 minutes, and power a color TV for 20 minutes.

• The amazing thing about glass is that it can be recycled forever.

Before putting jars and bottles in the recycling bin, rinse them, remove any lids and tops, and sort them into clear, green, and brown glass.

A used aluminum can is recycled and back on the grocery store shelf as a new can, in as little as 60 days! It's up to you to take action—recycle them.

OVER TO YOU

• Do you really need all those fizzy drinks? The answer is NO. Switch to a reusable, refillable bottle of tap water instead.

• Buy fresh fruit and vegetables, not canned. Don't let your family stock cupboards with cans of fruit and soup that never see the light of day.

Instead of towers of trash on the surface of the planet, we are in danger of ending up with towers of trash underground!

No.27: No One Wants A Six-Pack

When you buy canned drinks, are they held together by plastic holders? Do they have metal tabs to open them? If so, cut up the six-pack holders before disposing of them. Separate the metal tabs from cans completely and crush the cans flat before they go in the recycling bin. Animals and birds die from being trapped in or strangled by six-pack holders and cans.

No.28: Devise A Recycling System

Take a trip to your local garbage and recycling center. Make a note of what is thrown away and what can be recycled. In most countries, recyclable materials include glass, cans, plastic, paper, and cardboard. In some areas people are even encouraged to recycle clothing and shoes.

OVER TO YOU

Make it your job to set up a recycling system tailor-made for your household:

• Find out which materials are recycled in your area. Check whether they are collected from your house or whether you have to take them to a collection point.
• Write a list of all the items your household must recycle from now on. Make sure everyone reads it and then stick it up near your household bins.
• Some local communities provide special bins and bags for different categories of recyclable materials. If your town doesn't do this, you can make a selection of labeled boxes for each category of material. Again, make sure everyone knows what goes where.
• Monitor your family's recycling efforts closely.

No.29: Swap Shop

When was the last time you cleared out the toys, books, computer games, CDs, or DVDs you just didn't want anymore? Before buying any new ones, make sure you recycle the old ones. Unless they are broken beyond repair, DO NOT put them in the bin. Add them to a garage sale, give them to a thrift store, or why not sell them on eBay or at a flea market and make some money?

Alternatively, get DVDs and books from the library, or swap your unwanted stuff with things your friends no longer want. Someone else's unwanted goods may be your lucky find!

No.30: Reuse And Recycle Paper

Do you know what we throw away the most of? The answer is cardboard. The average person uses and disposes of the equivalent of seven trees a year.

This is crazy, because reusing and recycling paper is something that we can all do very easily—and it works. Moreover, making recycled paper instead of cutting down trees to make new paper uses 64% less energy and 58% less water.

OVER TO YOU

Here's how to reduce the amount of paper your family uses:

- Always use both sides of a piece of paper and use scraps for shopping lists.
- Get your family to use a chalkboard to leave messages for one another instead of sticky notes.
- Always print on both sides of a sheet of paper. Put an empty box beside your computer's printer to collect old printouts for reuse.
- Buy as many of your books as you can from flea markets or in secondhand shops.
- Always try to buy things made from recycled paper, such as toilet paper, paper towels, writing paper, wrapping paper, and notepads.

• Share books and magazines with your friends.
• Tear up wastepaper items such as dirty kitchen towels and add them to your compost bin. (Newspaper can go in, too, but beware of adding glossy magazines whose inks may contain nasty toxins.)
• Every single newspaper, sheet of paper, or cardboard that can't be reused or composted must go into the recycling box. Did you know that if we recycled all our newspapers, we would save about 250 million trees a year?

No. 31: Cut Out The Cards

It's wonderful to get a card from faraway family and friends, but do we really need all those birthday and holiday cards? Every year hundreds of thousands of trees are chopped down just to make holiday cards, and billions of those cards get put in the trash right after.

OVER TO YOU

• Use your computer to design greeting cards. Don't print them out, e-mail them. This saves paper, saves the fuel the post office uses to deliver them, and saves you money on stamps. If you aren't feeling creative or inspired, lots of Web sites offer ready-made e-cards with music and pictures.

• If you really want to give a card to someone in your family or class at school, suggest presenting one card and getting everyone to sign it. This avoids lots of individual cards and envelopes.

No.32: Recycle Your Shoes

Put an old sneaker on the compost heap, and see just how long it takes to decompose . . .

. . . on second thought, don't. You might find a family of bugs living in it, but you would have to stare at it for a long, long time to see it decompose. Now think of the millions of sneakers and other shoes that get dumped in landfill sites every day. In the U.S. alone, shoppers purchase almost eight pairs of new shoes every year.

OVER TO YOU

• Many shoes that are thrown away have little wrong with them. Make sure you take good-as-new or hardly worn sneakers to friends, the thrift stores, or a

What happens to the shoes put in the clothing donation bin?

Some are sent abroad. Others are used in programs like the one set up in 1993 by the sports company Nike, called Reuse-A-Shoe. Old sports shoes are ground up to create a material which is used to make running tracks, court surfaces, and children's playgrounds.

clothing donation bin. Why not get everyone at school to collect unwanted shoes and sneakers? Before you send your shoes anywhere, tie them together so they stay in pairs.

No.33: Better Batteries

Most standard batteries contain hazardous substances that may leak into the soil if they end up in landfill sites. Invest in rechargeable batteries with a charger. They can be used again and again before they need to be disposed of.

No. 34: When Is It Cool To Be An Old Bag?

Shopping bags made from a plastic called polyethylene are the single biggest polluters of our planet. About 100 billion plastic bags are thrown away in the USA every year, and in the UK the average person uses 134 bags every year.

FACT FILE

- Most people throw away a plastic bag after using it for just three minutes.

- If every shopper used one fewer bag each month, it would save hundreds of millions of bags each year.

- Up to a million sea creatures are killed every year by plastic bags and other garbage thrown in the sea.

- Plastic bags can cause floods by blocking drainage systems.

- In some countries, the rainwater that pools in dumped plastic bags can be a breeding ground for malaria-carrying mosquitoes.

OVER TO YOU

• Buy your household some canvas bags, and make sure nobody hits the supermarket and stores without them.
• Buy loose fruit and vegetables, not stuff that has been put in Styrofoam trays wrapped in plastic. Then make sure you don't undo all your good work by putting them in a plastic bag—they can go straight in your shopping cart.
• If you do take a plastic bag home, make sure you reuse it next time you go shopping.

It's soooo much better to use paper bags instead of plastic bags.

Duh!
No. In fact it takes more than four times as much energy to manufacture a paper bag as it does to manufacture a plastic bag.

No.35: Refill Not Refuse

Did you know that a third of all the trash in garbage dumps is old packaging?

Companies are developing plastics that will decompose, made from sugar and other carbohydrates. These rot away within months of being buried. Unfortunately, these cost a lot more money to produce. So we need to avoid packaging as much as possible.

OVER TO YOU

• Look out for products that come in containers that can be refilled. This means that you can use the same container again and again.

• Why not buy your family some travel cups that they can get filled in a coffee shop instead of being given Styrofoam cups?

• Don't buy plastic disposable items, such as cameras, plastic razors, picnic plates, and cutlery. They all end up in landfill sites. Make sure you buy things that will last.

• If you can't avoid packaging, choose cardboard rather than plastic.

No.36: Recycle Your Cell Phone

Americans throw away more than 130 million cell phones every year. Only 5% of these phones are recycled. The rest end up in landfill sites where the metals they contain (including gold and silver) are wasted. They also contain toxic substances, such as cadmium, mercury, lead, and arsenic, which can leak into the soil. Ingesting just small quantities of lead can damage our kidneys, liver, brain, heart, blood, and nerves, cause memory loss, and affect behavior and reproduction.

OVER TO YOU

• If your phone is still working—don't upgrade it.
• When you do want to upgrade, contact a charity, such as Oxfam, who will reuse or recycle your phone. Alternatively, find a site on the Web that will recycle your phone and send you money for it.
• Why not start a collection at school for old phones? You'll be amazed how many phones are hidden at the bottom of drawers in every household.

Did you know that leakage from just one cell phone battery can pollute 158,000 gallons of water?

No.37: Recycle Your Ink Cartridges And Computers

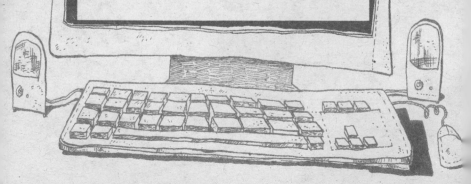

• Don't let anyone you know throw away a computer just because they think it is out of date. Someone else might be glad to have it.

• If you do get rid of a computer, take it to your local trash and recycling center so it is disposed of properly. Computers contain dangerous chemicals that may leak into the soil.

• Don't forget to recycle your ink cartridges, too. Leaking ink can also pollute the environment, and the plastic they're made of will take many years to decompose.

• Look on the Web for charitable organizations that collect and recycle printer cartridges, thereby keeping them out of landfill sites. The money they raise is used to help the world's poorest and most vulnerable people.

No.38: Reuse Your Garbage Creatively

Here are some ideas of how to be a creative recycler.

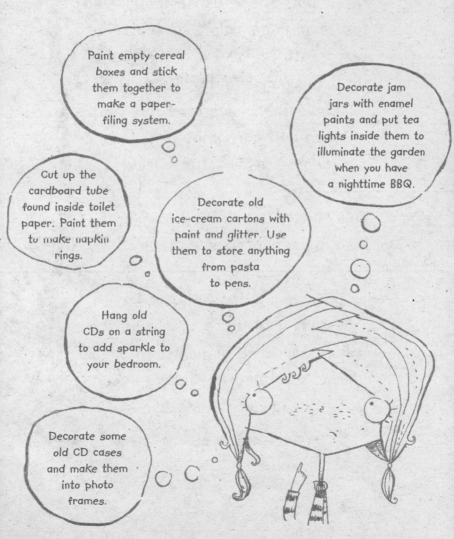

Paint empty cereal boxes and stick them together to make a paper-filing system.

Decorate jam jars with enamel paints and put tea lights inside them to illuminate the garden when you have a nighttime BBQ.

Cut up the cardboard tube found inside toilet paper. Paint them to make napkin rings.

Decorate old ice-cream cartons with paint and glitter. Use them to store anything from pasta to pens.

Hang old CDs on a string to add sparkle to your bedroom.

Decorate some old CD cases and make them into photo frames.

Poisonous emissions are destroying the planet. These emissions include the toxic chemicals that factories pump into the sky and the waste that is dumped into rivers. They include the gases given off by planes and cars that transport people around the world.

The amount of emissions polluting our planet increases every day.

You need to look at the way your family treats and travels the planet, to ensure that you don't leave our Earth a dirtier place than you found it.

Chapter Five
Stop Polluting The Planet

No.39: Save Our Oceans

Our seas are becoming dangerously polluted with harmful chemicals and sewage. Marine plants and animals and even people who are just paddling at the seaside are suffering.

FRIGHTENING FACTS

- Oil spills dump an average of 29,000 tons (27,000 metric tons) of oil into the world's oceans every year.

- Sweden has 85,000 lakes; over 21,000 are polluted by acid rain (see page 78).

- Oil slicks are a major hazard to marine life.

- Dangerous chemicals from farming and industry are washed into rivers and waterways and end up in the sea.

- Sewage pumped into the sea washes up on beaches, making them unsafe to play on.

OVER TO YOU

Play your own part in keeping the seaside safe:

• Make sure that you don't leave any garbage behind you on the beach. Always take it home with you. Plastic bags and balloons, for example, are a danger to sea creatures. If they blow into the water they can be mistaken for food by marine life. Once eaten, these materials may fool the creatures into thinking their stomachs are full and they will starve.

• If you live near the sea, join a conservation group that gets together to clean up beaches. Your local library will have more information.

No.40: Save Our School

Set up a club at school to protect a local area of natural beauty. If there isn't an obvious area of natural beauty nearby, such as a river, a forest, or a beach, why not choose to protect your school playground?

Organize teams of friends to clear the litter people have dropped. Talk to your school's principal about using environmentally friendly ways of killing pests and weeds. Perhaps you could explain how much water is wasted by watering the grass during a hot summer.

No.41: Reduce Acid Rain

When power stations, factories, and cars burn fuel, greenhouse gases escape into the air. Some of these gases react with droplets of water in clouds to form sulfuric and nitric acids, which is how we get acid rain.

ACID RAIN FACT FILE:

• Acid rain is polluting lakes and rivers and killing wildlife. In Scandinavia, lakes which seem crystal clear are known as "dead lakes." Thanks to acid rain they now contain no living creatures or plants.

• Acid rain destroys trees and forests. It can increase the acidity of soil so that trees can't grow. It can dissolve and wash away vital nutrients and minerals in the soil. It can damage the waxy protective coating of leaves, which may prevent them from being able to photosynthesize properly.

• Acid rain is eroding ancient statues and damaging buildings—it will even damage your car if it is left outside.

The best way for you to help with acid rain is to take all the advice in this book about saving fuel and conserving energy.

Oh, and if you do leave the car at home, better put it in the garage in case it rains acid!

No.42: Get To Know Your Family

About 12% of the greenhouse gases that cause global warming are produced by transportation. So it's time to monitor your family's traveling habits and transportation decisions.

Start with your family car. Watch your parents' driving habits. Do they drive smoothly? Do they turn off the engine when they stop for more than 30 seconds at traffic lights? Is the trunk empty of everything but essentials? All these sensible driving practices can significantly reduce the amount of fuel a car consumes.

You must also tell your parents to get their car serviced regularly. A smooth-running engine emits fewer nasty substances. If all car owners serviced their vehicles regularly, millions of pounds of CO_2 would be eliminated from the atmosphere. Make sure they get the mechanic to check that the tires are properly inflated, because underinflated tires use up more energy. Make sure they check that the air-conditioning system is not leaking dangerous chemicals into the air.

Get your parents to help fill in the questionnaire on the next page to see how green they are when it comes to cars. The more times they answer YES, the more they need to change their driving habits.

	YES	NO
1. Does your family own a car that only does a mile/gallon of gas?	☐	☐
2. Does it seem like the car is always in use?	☐	☐
3. Is your car more than five years old?	☐	☐
4. Does your family make a lot of short trips in the car that could be avoided?	☐	☐
5. Has the air-conditioning system not been checked since the car was bought?	☐	☐
6. Do the drivers in your family drive at high speeds and rev the engine impatiently when stuck in traffic jams?	☐	☐
7. Do your parents leave the car's engine running while you are grabbing your bags and piling into the car in the morning?	☐	☐
8. Do your parents forget to get the car serviced regularly?	☐	☐
9. Has it been over a week since your parents checked the pressure in their tires?	☐	☐
10. Is your car trunk full of lots of unnecessary stuff—like Dad's golf clubs, beach chairs, backpacks, and so on?	☐	☐

No.43: Car Wash

Don't let your parents take the car to the automatic car wash. It uses a huge amount of water, electricity, and chemicals to do something that you could achieve with a bucket and sponge.

Maybe washing the car by hand could be the punishment you hand out to members of the family who commit any of the eco-crimes described in this book.

No.44: Get On Your Bike Or Put Your Best Foot Forward

Bicycling is a 100% green way to travel. Apart from the resources used in its manufacture and disposal, a bike never again damages the planet. Oh, and it's a great way of getting lots of exercise.

If you don't have a bike, ask around to see if anyone has outgrown theirs, or check out a flea market or eBay. Get a friend to check that your bike is roadworthy before you ride it.

WHEELY USEFUL TIPS

- Always wear a helmet and suitable clothing. After dark, use lights and wear reflective clothing.
- Learn traffic codes and rules.
- Never listen to music while cycling on roads.
- Don't ride on sidewalks.

Did you know that riding a bike at a reasonable speed burns 400 calories an hour? Driving a car for an hour burns only 58 calories.

Walking is a 100% cheap, green, and clean way of traveling. Whenever possible, make it your family mission to walk rather than drive—on short journeys to school or the local shops.

If your parents need further persuading, remind them that they won't need to spend ten minutes looking for a parking place or pay to park the car.

The diagram below compares how many tons of CO_2 are produced in a year by a daily ten-mile journey when it is made in a car, in a bus, on a train, and on foot.

CAR
0.86 tons

BUS
0.6 tons

TRAIN
0.3 tons

FOOT
zero tons

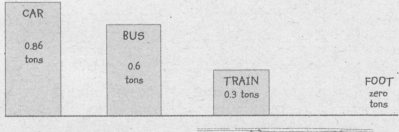

This section looks at the plants
and animals that inhabit the planet.
They need saving, too.

Right now, more species of animals
and insects are disappearing
from our planet than ever before.
Some scientists think as many
as a million species of plants and
animals are currently in danger of
becoming extinct. Most of them
will disappear as a result of the
things human beings do.

Make sure you are not one of the
planet's most wanted eco-criminals.

Chapter Six
Save All
Species

No.45: Sponsor A Rain Forest

Do you want to know a really, really scary fact?

Without rain forests, all life on this planet may become unsustainable. Due to tree clearance and logging, rain forests are being destroyed at a truly horrifying rate—about the equivalent of two football fields every second.

Almost half of Earth's rain forests are already gone for good, and at this rate, by 2060, there will be none remaining.

Get everyone you know to sponsor a rain forest.

Check out the Web for organizations that are trying to save rain forests. If your friends ask why they should get involved, tell them to check out the facts below.

FOREST FACTS

- Tropical rain forests are the single greatest producer of the air that we breathe.

- Tropical rain forests absorb huge quantities of poisonous CO_2. In doing so, they stabilize the world's climate.

- The clearing and burning of our rain forests accounts for up to 25% of the greenhouse gases produced by humans.

- Rain forests influence weather by controlling rainfall and the evaporation of water from soil.

- Rain forests are home not only to indigenous tribespeople, but also to two-thirds of all the living species on the planet (about 50 to 70 million different life forms).

- Over one-third of the medicines in the developed world have ingredients that derive from rain-forest plants. For example, the rosy periwinkle of Madagascar is used to treat childhood leukemia. These ingredients would disappear if the rain forests were destroyed.

No.46: Don't Pick Wild Plants

Many wild flowers and plants have disappeared, or are in danger of disappearing. One of the main causes of this is the clearing of woodlands, hedgerows, and forests to make way for agriculture. However, the picking of wildflowers is also a huge problem. Many plants, from orchids to mosses, are now protected, because in the past people have picked too many and have dramatically reduced their numbers.

Never pick wild plants and flowers when you are out walking, and tell your friends and family to do the same.

No.47: Don't Buy Fur

If you buy anything that looks furry, check that it is man-made. The fur of many animals—including cats and dogs—currently ends up in pom-poms, fur-lined boots, fur-trimmed coats and gloves, and toys such as animal figurines.

Be aware, too, that labels can be misleading. An item made with fur described as imitation may not be fake after all. Don't chance it, don't buy it.

NOT FURRY NICE FACTS

• An estimated two million cats and dogs are killed each year in China. Many are skinned alive.

• Over 30 million animals a year are killed on fur farms.

• It requires the fur of 100 chinchillas to make one human-sized fur coat.

• In spite of a government ban on the killing of young seals and pups, 268,921 seals were killed off the coast of Canada in 1996.

No.48: Adopt An Animal

Some of our favorite animals are in danger of becoming extinct—because of us. Rare animals are killed for their skins, tusks, and horns, and even for sport . . . gross! Wildlife organizations are doing as much as they can to protect these animals, but your help is needed.

OVER TO YOU

For a small amount of money each month, you could help to save a panda, a gorilla, an elephant, or a rhinoceros—and you won't even have to feed or clean it! If you can't afford this yourself, ask if you can adopt an animal for your birthday or a holiday present.

Once you have chosen your animal and arranged to pay your donation, you should expect to receive an adoption certificate and information all about YOUR animal.

No.49: Go To The Zoo

Zoos and safari parks are committed to saving endangered species, and your entrance fee alone will help to keep an animal safe and fed.

Make sure you support your local zoo or wildlife park by paying it a visit. Find out about the animals looked after and bred there. Remember they are not just there for you to look at, however. They are there because we have destroyed their homes and habitats, and have hunted others near to extinction. Without your help, many of our favorite animals will no longer be seen anywhere on this earth.

No.50: Tune In To Tuna

Fishermen have known for a long time that tuna fish like to swim beneath groups of dolphins. As dolphins are easier to spot, fishermen often cast their nets around them to catch the tuna fish swimming below.

It is thought that in the last 50 years, around seven million dolphins have drowned as a result of becoming tangled up in nets.

Dolphins are still being caught up in fishing nets today. The good news is that in 1990 the "Dolphin-Safe" label was introduced to cans of tuna, promising that no dolphins had been harmed in catching the fish. So check the labeling on any can of tuna that you buy. If you can't see the words "Dolphin-Safe," leave it on the supermarket shelf.

By now you should be well on the way to making your home a greener, cleaner place. However, it is very important that everyone you know makes the same effort.

Now you need to tell other people about all the things they can do to make a difference.

Chapter Seven
Spread The Word

Round Up Some Eco-warriors

Word of mouth is the best way to change the world. Tell everyone at school what you have found out about energy saving and recycling. Discuss with them ways your school can reduce waste, recycle things, and protect the environment.

Why not set up an ecology club and put out a newsletter telling people about the green projects you are working on?

Share ideas of how to go green with people by including information on your own Web site or MySpace page.

Bigger Is Better

Saving the planet is a lot of work for one person. Make sure you recycle this book by giving it to all your friends and family. Alternatively, sit them down and talk about the information you have read in this book and what can be done to help the planet. Tell them to spread the word, too. Together you can make a bigger difference.

Make A Friend Across The Globe

There are over 6,500,000,000 people on Earth, so there are plenty of new friends to be made and converted to your green cause. Let's face it, our planet needs all the friends it can get.

See if your school can correspond with a school somewhere else in the world. You could e-mail the pupils there. Find out what life is like in their country. What sort of things do they do to help the planet? Exchange ideas and plans. Remember, together you can save the world.

NOTES

All that's left for you to do is to sign the planet pledge below and act on all the things you have read about in this book. Copy out the pledge and get all the members of your family to read the book and sign it, too.

MY PLEDGE TO THE PLANET

I promise faithfully to try to remember all the things that I have read in this book and to remember to do them.

I will not be responsible for destroying the planet's future by doing things that make my life easier today.

Signed by ....

Witnessed by ....

MY FAMILY'S PLEDGE
TO THE PLANET

We promise faithfully to try to remember all the things that we have read in this book and to remember to do them.

We will not be responsible for destroying the planet's future by doing things that make our lives easier today.

Signed by ....

Signed by ....

Signed by ....

Signed by ....

Witnessed by ....

USEFUL WEB SITES

Here are some great green Web sites to check out.

U.S. Environmental Protection Agency
www.epa.gov

Kids Recycle!
www.kidsrecycle.org

Recycle City
www.epa.gov/recyclecity

Environmental Kids Club
www.epa.gov/kids/

Tike The Penguin
tiki.oneworld.net

Greenpeace
www.greenpeace.org

INDEX